iving in

naica

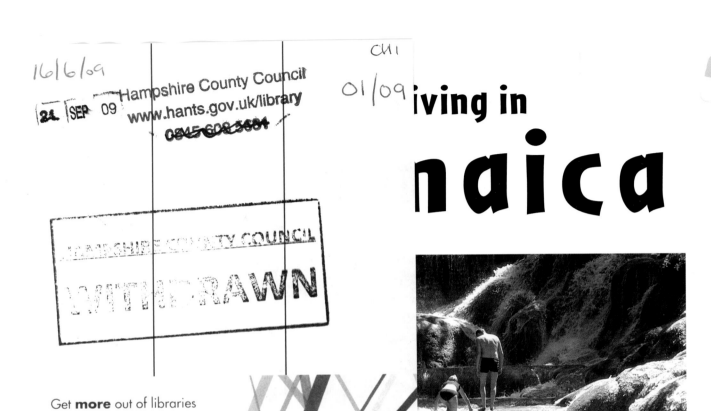

nd photographed
udy Bastyra

W

First published in 2002 by
Franklin Watts,
338 Euston Rd
London NW1 3BH

Franklin Watts Australia,
Level 17/207 Kent Street
Sydney, NSW 2000
Copyright © Franklin Watts 2002

Series editor: Ruth Thomson
Series designer: Edward Kinsey
Consultant: Karen Carpenter, Lecturer in
Psychology, University of the West Indies

Additional photographs: Eye Ubiquitous: cover, 6(c), 19(l),
20(c), 23(l); James Davis Worldwide: 8(c); Jamaican
Information Service: 28(l and r); Jamaican Tourist Board:
5(br), 9(tl), 13(bl), 14(tl and bl); Cookie Kinkaid: title page,
8(br), 9(tr); Half Moon Hotel: 4(c); J. Wray and Nephew
15(tr and br); David Hampton: 3, 10(c), 13(br), 17(tr, bl,
br), 21(br), 24(tr,br), 25, 27(br), 28 (tr), 29(tr, br), 30.

A CIP catalogue record for this book is
available from the British Library
Dewey Classification 917.292
ISBN 978 0 7496 6339 1

Printed in China

Franklin Watts is a division of Hachette Children's Books

*The author would like to thank the following people
and organisations for their help with this book:
Mavis Belasse, Bunny, Virginia Burke, Marilyn
Delevante, Carl Dennis, Mike Dennis, Ryan
Douglas, The Excelsior Pre-primary and Primary
schools, The Gleaner, Peta-Vonne and Yvonne
Golding, Venise Green, The Jamaican Information
Service in London, The Jamaican Tourist Board,
Junior Lodge, Ele Rickhams, St. Teresa's Prep.
School, Maxine Shroder, Carmen Tipling, Beverley
White, Evan Williams.*

Contents

This is Jamaica

Jamaica is an island in the Caribbean Sea, south of Cuba and west of Haiti.

It has numerous mountains, rivers, waterfalls and beaches, as well as forests and woodlands. Its original name, *Xaymaca*, means 'land of wood and water'.

△**Fresh fish**
Fishing provides food for the island.

▷**Half Moon Bay**
The island's wide, sandy beaches attract more than a million tourists each year.

△**The Blue Mountains**
Coffee is grown on these mountains just north of Kingston.

Fact Box

Capital: Kingston
Population: 2.7 million
Official Languages: English and Jamaican Creole (Patwa)
Main religions: Christianity and Rastafarianism
Highest mountain: Blue Mountains Peak (2,256m)
Longest river: Black River (70km)
Biggest cities: Kingston, Montego Bay
Currency: Jamaican dollar

Jamaica's national motto is: 'Out of one, many people.'

▷Bamboo Avenue
Bamboo grows well in Jamaica's tropical climate.

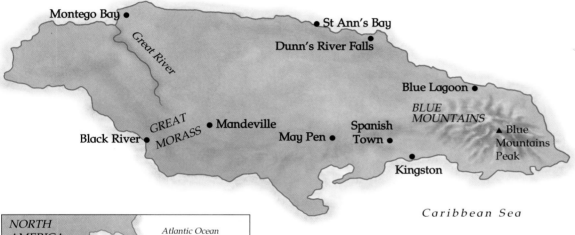

Montego Bay •
St Ann's Bay •
Dunn's River Falls •
Great River
Blue Lagoon •
BLUE MOUNTAINS
GREAT
MORASS • Mandeville
Spanish Town •
▲ Blue Mountains Peak
Black River •
May Pen •
Kingston •

Caribbean Sea

NORTH AMERICA
Atlantic Ocean
DOMINICAN REPUBLIC
CUBA
HAITI
Pacific Ocean
JAMAICA
Caribbean Sea
SOUTH AMERICA

▷St Ann's Bay
There are sheltered bays and coves all along the north coast. In 1494, the explorer Christopher Columbus landed at this bay, looking for gold.

Kingston – the capital

Kingston, the capital of Jamaica, is a big city that sprawls along the south-east coast. It is bordered on two sides by the Blue Mountains.

The city is home to the Government, big businesses, banks, major shops and theatres. It also has one of the world's largest deep-water harbours.

△**Soldiers**
Soldiers help the police keep the peace in times of emergency.

△**Downtown**
Downtown is the centre of Kingston and the old city. Many people work in offices here.

◁**New Kingston**
New Kingston is a business district, with modern high-rise hotels, banks and office buildings, as well as houses.

◁Heroes' Park

This memorial honours soldiers who fought alongside the British in the two World Wars (1914-18 and 1939-45).

▷National heroes

Other memorials in the park honour Jamaica's seven national heroes – Bustamante, Nanny, Bogle, Sharp, Manley, Garvey and Gordon.

Sir Alexander Bustamante, Jamaica's first Prime Minister

◁Devon House

George Stiebel, Jamaica's first black millionaire, built this home in 1740. It is now a museum with shops, an ice-cream parlour and restaurants in the grounds.

7

Famous sights

The famous sights of Jamaica are both natural and historic. The Spanish came to Jamaica in 1494. The British captured the island in 1655 and brought African slaves to work on their tobacco and sugar plantations. They ruled until independence in 1962.

Several plantation houses are now museums and show how both slaves and plantation managers lived.

△Heritage Park
This life-sized model of an Afro-Jamaican house is made of wattle and daub. It is in the Maima Seville Great House and Heritage Park.

▷Port Royal
This town was the pirate capital of the Caribbean. It was once the richest place in the New World. It was destroyed by an earthquake in 1692.

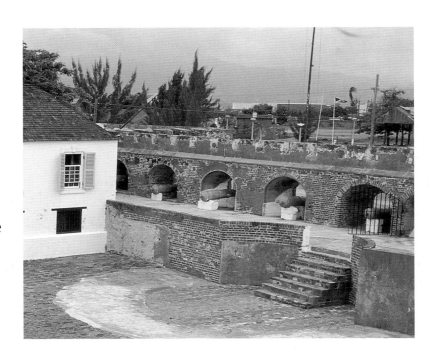

△Rose Hall
The most famous plantation house in Jamaica has been restored to its original state. A witch is said to haunt it.

◁**Blue Lagoon**
This very deep lagoon is fed by fresh-water springs. It changes colour, from deep blue to intense green, all through the day.

▷**Dunn's River Falls**
This is the largest and most famous of the many falls that are found on the island. Many international films are made here.

◁**Animal and bird life**
About 300 crocodiles live by the mangroves (tropical trees) in the Black River. More than 100 species of birds live in the wetlands of the Great Morass that surround the river.

Living in cities

There are two large cities in Jamaica – Kingston and Montego Bay. A third of the population lives in Kingston. Montego Bay, a much smaller city, is a tourist resort on the north coast. It has some of the most luxurious hotels and shops on the island. Many Jamaicans find work here in the tourist industry.

Jamaica 90c

YELLOW-BILLED PARROT

$1.10 FIRE – NEVILLE GARRICK 50th Anniversary of the Birth of Bob Marley JAMAICA

Jamaican stamps

◁△**The post office**
There are very few post boxes, so people mail letters at the post office. They can collect post here as well, from their own, individual mailbox.

◁**Tivoli Gardens**
This area of housing is one of the most dangerous places in Kingston. There are often fights here between local gangs.

▽**Water hydrants**
Water hydrants are a common sight all over Kingston.
The fire service uses them in emergencies.

▽Office work

The head offices of major industries, such as banks, insurance, distilleries, mining, cement and flour mills are found in Kingston.

Working in the city

Country people are increasingly moving to the cities to find work. Young people come to learn a trade, or to work in offices, hotels and hospitals.

△Street selling

In many areas of town, street traders sell food they have bought from farmers.

▷Pan chicken

Cooked chicken is sold by the roadside. It is grilled over charcoal in converted oil drums.

Living in the country

Jamaicans call anywhere outside the cities 'country'. Some villages are tiny and remote. Others, on main roads, have a church, a general shop and a bar. When Jamaicans return to the island after many years working abroad, they usually build their new homes in the countryside.

△Squatting
People often live in houses on abandoned land that doesn't belong to them. This is called 'squatting on captured land'.

▷Village houses
In the country, there is space for people to add on new rooms to their houses, as their family grows in size.

△Chattel house
Village houses are often made of wood. The overhanging verandah gives shade from the sweltering sun.

▷Clothes washing

Not all country people have running water. They wash their clothes in a nearby stream or river.

▽The market

Once a week, country people go to their nearest market to buy food, clothes and household goods.

'Picka-peppa' sauce

Honey

Hot pepper sauce

Tinned ackee (tropical fruit)

Tropical fruit sticks

Cookies

Guava jelly

△A village shop

Village shops sell lots of different items, such as tinned and packet foods, as well as kerosine and matches.

Working in the country

In the country, people raise sheep, cows and goats or grow crops, such as bananas, sugar cane, coffee and vegetables. Some people mine bauxite, used to make aluminium, or work in food or drink factories. Hotels, restaurants and tourist attractions on the coast employ a great many people, too.

△Vegetable farming

Vegetables are grown to sell locally. Some restaurants and hotels pay farmers to grow certain vegetables, such as peppers and courgettes.

▷Goat rearing

Farmers raise goats for their meat. Curry goat and *mannish water* (goat broth) are both very popular dishes.

◁Bananas

Bananas are grown as a cash crop. They are picked before they are fully ripe. They turn yellow as they ripen, on their way to other countries.

▽Village crafts

Some villages earn a living through crafts.
This village makes hand-made brooms with
palm leaves and wood from local trees.

Country industries

Food and drink processing factories
are mainly in the country, near where
the crops are produced. These provide
jobs for local people.

△Sugar cane

Sugar cane is an
important crop. The
cane is pressed to
extract its juice. This is
fermented and made
into rum or vodka.

▷Rum barrels

Rum is put into barrels
and left for several
years to age, before it is
bottled. Rum is an
important Jamaican
export.

Shopping

Every city and town has a market, which takes place daily or weekly. Many places also have a supermarket. In the cities, there are indoor shopping malls and plazas, where a number of small shops are grouped around a car park. In tourist areas, there are smart boutiques selling clothes and souvenirs.

△**Coconut water**
Roadside coconut sellers cut off the top of green coconuts, so people can drink the water inside.

▷**Fresh peas**
This farmer has brought his gungo peas to sell on the street. Behind him, another street seller (*higgler*) has laid out clothes to sell.

▽**Hub caps**
Jamaicans like making their cars look smart. Hub caps are often sold in the open-air, like this.

△**Pots and pans**
These traditional, heavy 'Dutchy' cooking pots are made in Jamaica.

△**A furniture store**
Courts is the largest furniture store in Jamaica. It has branches all over the island. It also helps to raise money for schools.

▽**Fabric**
Many people in Jamaica make their own clothes. They buy fabric and thread at haberdashery shops.

△**A book shop**
Bookshops import books from America and Britain, as well as selling books published in Jamaica.

Two famous Jamaican stories

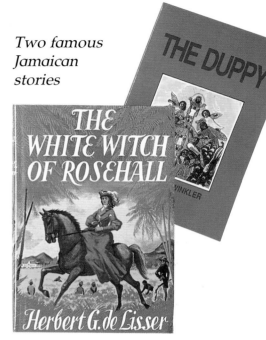

△**Jamaican money**
Jamaica's currency is dollars and cents.

17

On the move

Not everywhere on the island can be reached by car. It can take many hours to drive from one place to another, because most roads are so twisty.

Jamaicans drive on the left. They have a saying to remind visitors, 'Keep left and you'll always be right'.

△Motor bikes
Motor bikes are a popular form of transport. People often share rides.

▷Country roads
There are over 15,000km of roads, but only a quarter of them are paved. Many have pot holes after heavy rains.

▷New roads
New roads have helped to ease the traffic jams to and from the capital.

◁ Bus transport
Every town has a bus waiting area, usually near the main market or shopping centre.

▽ Cars
Many people own cars. They buy cheap, second-hand cars from abroad.

Buses and railways

A bus network links virtually every village in the country. Air-conditioned express buses carry office workers to and from Kingston. Cheaper, slower buses stop more frequently.

Jamaica used to have a passenger railway, but trains are now used only to transport bauxite to the port.

Religion

Religion plays an important role in the Jamaican way of life. Most Jamaicans are Christian. Each weekend, families go to church together to pray and meet their friends from the same parish. There are many different kinds of church in each parish, such as Baptist, Methodist and Seventh Day Adventist.

△**Saying grace**
Families often say grace at mealtimes, thanking God for providing their food.

△**Going to church**
People dress in their best clothes to go to church.

◁**Church services**
Singing is an important part of church services. Many churches have choirs. In this service someone is being baptised.

△▽Rasta hats
Rastafarians twist their hair into long lengths called dreadlocks as a symbol of their beliefs. A rasta hat is larger than usual, in order to cover the dreadlocks.

The teachings of Haile Selassie

A Rasta hat (a tam)

△▷Rastafarians
Rastafarians believe that the late emperor of Ethiopia, Haile Selassie, is their living God.

A CD by Bob Marley, the Reggae singer, Jamaica's most famous Rastafarian

△Seventh Day Adventists
These Christians believe in a very simple life, good food and regular exercise. Their holy day lasts from sundown on Friday until sundown on Saturday.

21

Family life

In Jamaica, everyone related to you is considered part of your close family. Although some fathers and mothers do not live together, everyone in the family helps to bring up the children. Sometimes, when their parents go abroad to work, children are looked after by grandmothers and aunties.

△**Children**
Children are considered a great blessing. The more children you have, the more blessed you are.

◁**Extended families**
Some families include three generations living together.

◁Rastafarians
Rastafarian women are expected to be modest and humble.

▷Close families
Many families live near to their relatives. Cousins often play together.

Working mothers
Many women go out to work as well as bringing up their family. Those who can afford it employ helpers to run their homes and look after the children until they come home from work.

◁Fathers
Fathers play an active role in their children's lives. Fathers not married to their children's mothers are known as 'baby fathers'.

Time to eat

No one in Jamaica need ever go hungry. Plenty of fruit and vegetables grow in the fertile island soil. There is always a good supply of fish, chicken and pork. Most Jamaicans eat three hearty meals a day and one of them always includes rice.

They also drink a great many fresh fruit juices and nourishing food supplements.

Bammies

△**A fish dish**
Fried fish with hot peppers, onion rings and cassava bread (*bammy*) is sold by roadsides near the sea.

◁▽**Patties**
Patties are the national snack. These crescent-shaped pies are filled with minced beef, chicken or shrimp.

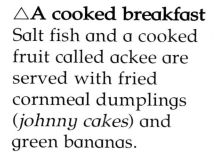

△**A cooked breakfast**
Salt fish and a cooked fruit called ackee are served with fried cornmeal dumplings (*johnny cakes*) and green bananas.

A patty

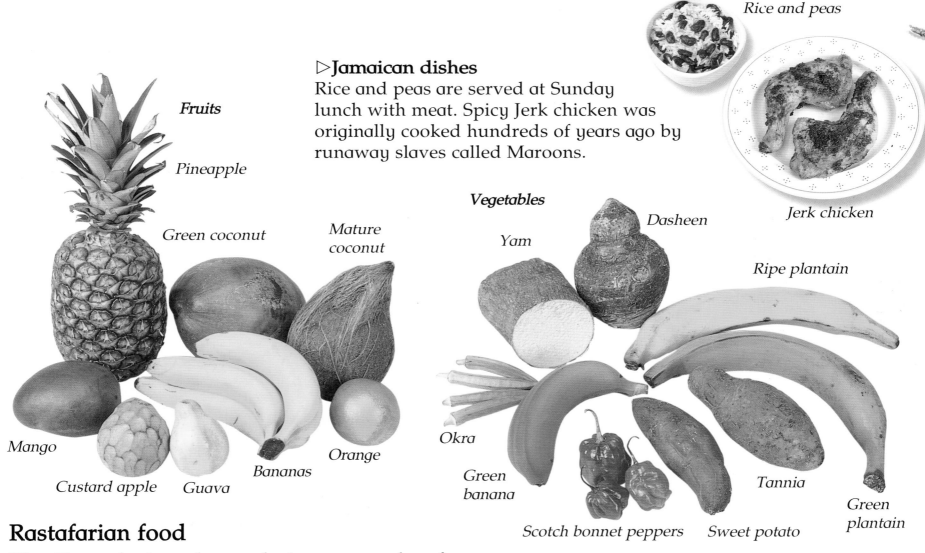

Fruits

Pineapple

Green coconut

Mature coconut

Mango

Custard apple

Guava

Bananas

Orange

▷Jamaican dishes

Rice and peas are served at Sunday lunch with meat. Spicy Jerk chicken was originally cooked hundreds of years ago by runaway slaves called Maroons.

Rice and peas

Jerk chicken

Vegetables

Yam

Dasheen

Ripe plantain

Okra

Green banana

Scotch bonnet peppers

Sweet potato

Tannia

Green plantain

Rastafarian food

The Rastafarians have their own style of cooking, called Ital. They are vegetarian and do not use many seasonings or salt. They believe in eating fresh, pure food.

◁Bun and cheese

A common Jamaican snack is a sandwich made from spiced bun and processed cheese.

School time

Jamaicans value education highly. Children have to go to school up to the age of 15. Some Jamaican families who live abroad have begun sending their children back to the island to be educated. They feel that schooling in Jamaica is better than elsewhere.

△**School hours**
School starts at 8am and finishes at 1.30pm. At about 10am, children wash their hands outside before their mid-morning snack.

△**Walk to school**
Most children who live in the country walk to school. The older children walk with their younger sisters or brothers.

◁**The school**
The classrooms at this school are built around a shady courtyard.

◁**School uniform**
Every school has a school uniform. Children wear a separate uniform for sports.

▷**Classroom**
There are between 20 and 30 children to a class. Both a teacher and a student teacher take many of the lessons.

Further education
Many pupils go on to further education after secondary school, as this will help them get a better job. They may go to a technical college, a teacher's training college, or to the universities in Kingston.

△**Religious education**
Children are taught how to behave. Sometimes bible stories are used.

△**Reading books**
English books include many poems and stories written about Jamaica.

77

Having fun

Jamaicans spend their leisure time on the beach, playing and following sport, watching TV, going to the cinema and listening to music.

No party is complete without dancing to the sound of Reggae music, which started in Jamaica.

▷The lottery
The lottery is so popular that it is drawn twice a week.

▽Dance
Jamaicans are very proud of their dance and music traditions.

▽Playing in the sea
Every weekend, the beaches are packed with families.

◁Cricket

Many boys want to become cricketers. If they cannot afford the real equipment, they make their own bat and use a small coconut as a cricket ball.

△The Reggae Boyz

Jamaicans are keen supporters of their national football team, the Reggae Boyz.

◁Football

Playing football is a favourite pastime for young Jamaican boys.

△ *The Children's Own*

This children's newspaper, written partly by children, is sent to schools throughout Jamaica.

Going further

Bob Marley

Bob Marley is Jamaica's most famous musician. There is a museum about him in Kingston. He died some years ago, but his music is still very popular.

Either listen to his music or read his lyrics and then design a Bob Marley CD cover. You can find out more about him at www.bobmarley.com.

Colourful birds

Jamaica has many bird species not found anywhere else in the world. These include the Jamaican Tody, the Jamaican Blackbird and the Orangequit. Choose one of these birds and write a report about it. Describe what the bird looks like, its habitat, and its feeding and nesting habits.

Treasure hunt

The fierce pirate, Captain Henry Morgan, buried some of his treasure in Jamaica.

Draw a map of Jamaica and mark the place where you think his treasure might be.

Websites

www.jamaicatravel.com

www.everytingjamaican.com/channels/theisland/index.asp

Glossary

Aluminium A light silvery metal, often used to make tinfoil or drinks cans.

Cash crop A crop that is grown for sale and not as food for a farmer.

Currency The money used by a country.

Distillery A place where alcohol is made.

Dreadlocks A hairstyle worn by Rastafarians, where long hair is twisted into tight braids.

Fermented Turned into alcohol.

Kerosine A paraffin oil used for heating and lamps.

Lagoon An area of sheltered coastal water separated from the sea by a sandbank or a coral reef.

New World The continents of North and South America and the islands around them, including those in the Caribbean. When Europeans first came to these places, it was like finding a new world.

Parish A Jamaican term for one of the 12 sub-divisions of the country's three counties – Cornwall, Middlesex and Surrey.

Patwa One of Jamaica's two languages, also known as Jamaican Creole. It is a mixture of Spanish, English and African languages.

Plantation Land planted with a single crop, such as coffee, sugar cane or bananas.

Population The total number of people living in a place.

Reggae music Popular music of the West Indies.

Slave A person who is legally owned by another.

Tropical Of the Tropics, the hot and often wet regions either side of the Equator, the imaginary line that runs round the Earth at its middle.

Wattle and daub A woven network of twigs covered with mud or clay, used for building.

Wetlands Swamps and other damp areas of land.

Index

Page numbers in *italics* refer to entries in the fact box, on the map or in the glossary.